Whitetail in the Woods

No part of this publication may be reproduced in whole or in part,
or stored in a retrieval system, or transmitted in any form or by any means,
electronic, mechanical, photocopying, recording, or otherwise,
without written permission from the author.

ISBN 979-8-218-04946-1

Copyright © 2022 by Savannah Robb
All rights reserved.
Printed in the USA.

Dedication

This book is dedicated to
Lacey & Levi,
and to all hunters, big & small.

Whitetail in the Woods

By
Savannah Robb

Illustrated by Moran Reudor

Today is the day,
The waiting is over.
Time to go hunt,
It's finally October!

I pull on my camouflage,
My orange hat, too.
We load the truck and drive,
Under the light of the moon.

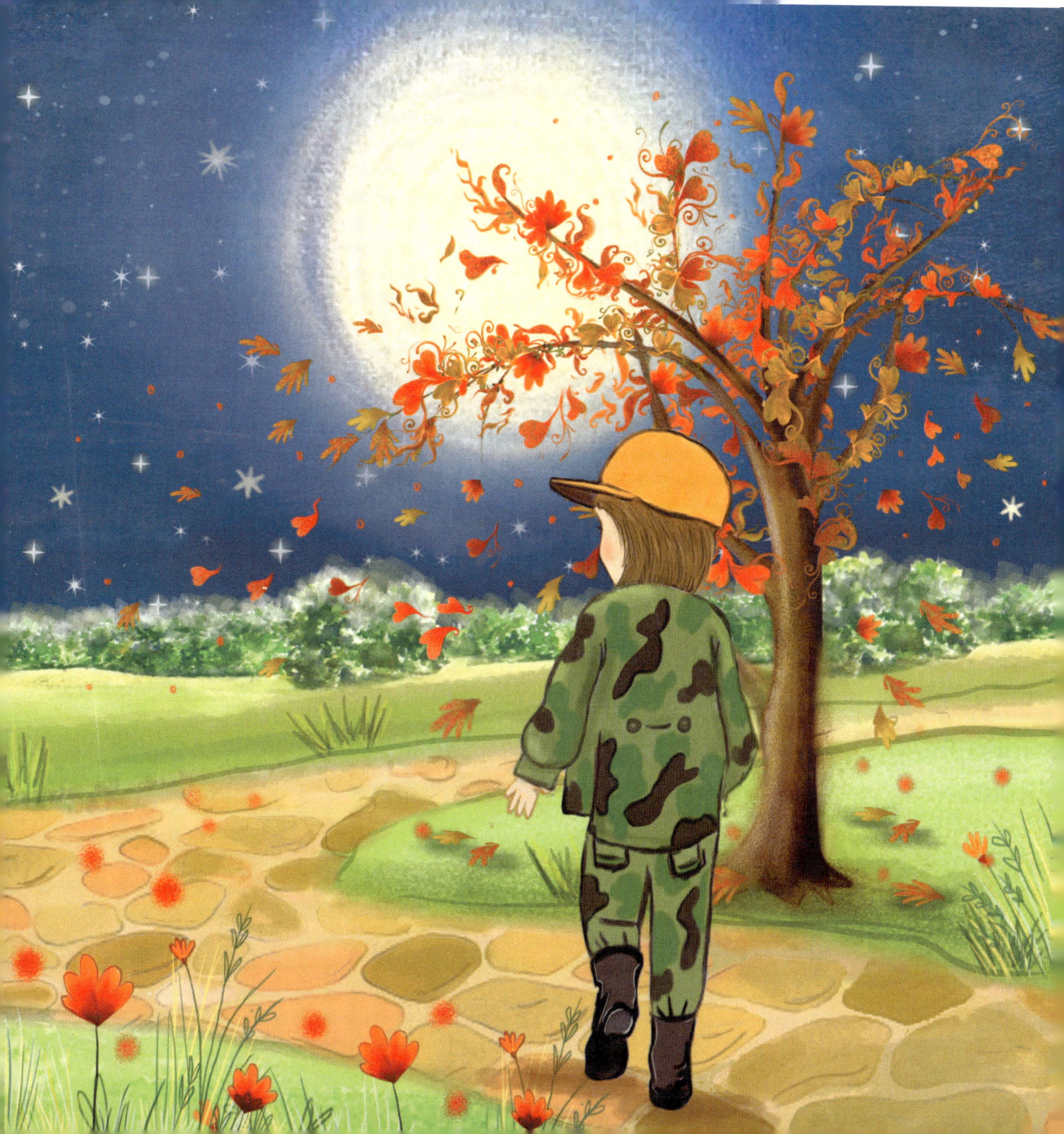

We get to the blind,
Is the rifle ready?
The safety is on,
I practice holding
　　it steady.

Let the waiting begin,
I hope we see deer!
I know I can do this,
With you sitting near.

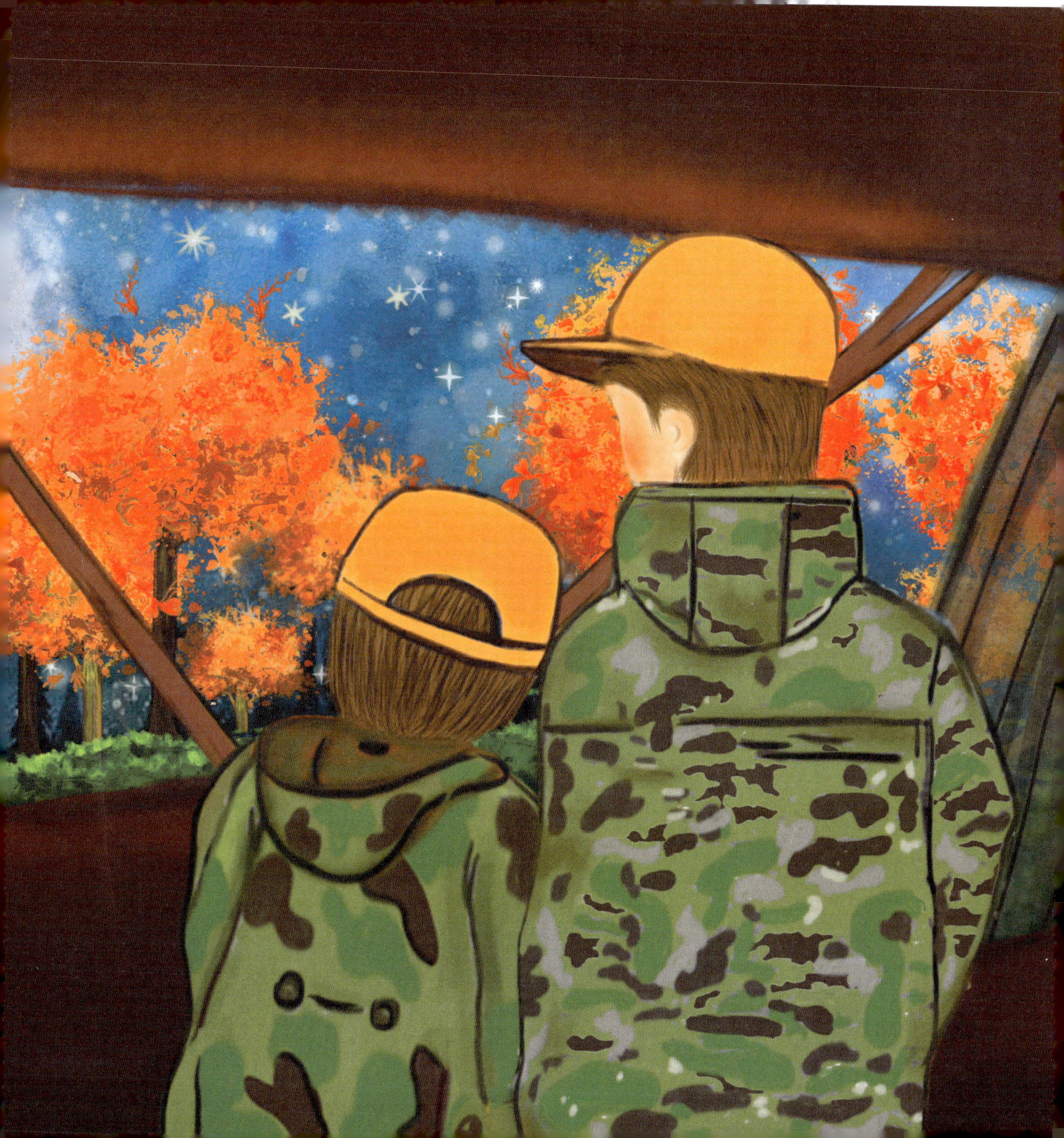

After some time,
We hear rustling leaves!
Shucks! No deer this time,
Just a squirrel jumping trees.

The sun is now up,
The woods fill with light.
Now would be perfect,
The conditions are right.

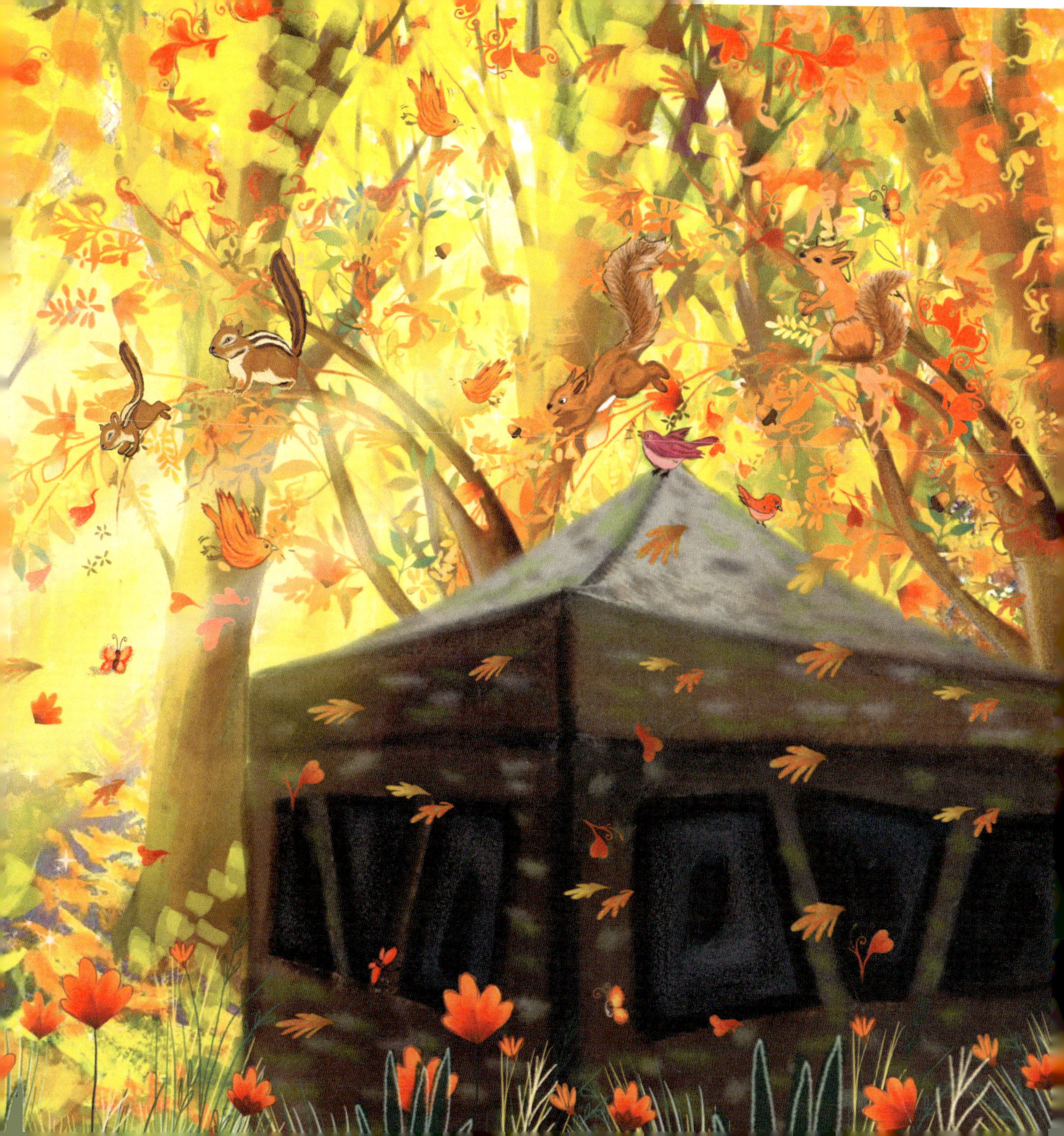

Then, something is moving!
It`s a buck! Look right there!
I peer through my scope,
And line up the crosshairs.

"Are you ready?" you ask.
"I've got him," I answer.
I pull the trigger and BOOM!
The sound echoes like thunder.

My heart is pounding,
As we look for my buck.
There he is! We found him!
Get him on the truck!

When we arrive home,
We celebrate my harvest!
We'll hang my deer's mount on the wall,
Between mom's and dad's largest.

When I hunt, I feel proud,
For the food I provide.
And I'm thankful for my family,
And time spent outside.

About the Author

Savannah Robb and her husband are proud of their family's hunting heritage and are eager to continue the tradition with their children. In her search for quality children's hunting books, she recognized the lack of stories featuring duos other than father and son. In this book, both boys and girls can imagine themselves as the one in the woods, and the accompanying adult could be a parent, grandparent, aunt, uncle or any other special person in a child's life.